Lutheranism 101
FOR KIDS

Julie and Scott Stiegemeyer

CONCORDIA PUBLISHING HOUSE · SAINT LOUIS

Lutheranism 101 Books

Lutheranism 101
Lutheranism 101: **THE COURSE**
Lutheranism 101 **FOR KIDS**
Lutheranism 101: **THE LORD'S SUPPER**
Lutheranism 101: **HOLY BAPTISM** *(2013)*
Lutheranism 101: **WORSHIP** *(2013)*

Copyright © 2012 Concordia Publishing House
3558 S. Jefferson Ave., St. Louis, MO 63118-3968
1-800-325-3040 • www.cph.org

Scripture quotations are from the ESV Bible® (The Holy Bible, English Standard Version®), copyright © 2001 by Crossway Bibles, a publishing ministry of Good News Publishers. Used by permission. All rights reserved.

Catechism quotations are from *Luther's Small Catechism with Explanation*, copyright © 1986, 1991 Concordia Publishing House. All rights reserved.

Material with the abbreviation *LSB* is from *Lutheran Service Book*, copyright © 2006 Concordia Publishing House. All rights reserved.

Quotation on page 28 is from *Lutheranism 101*, copyright © 2010 Concordia Publishing House. All rights reserved.

Interior images © Shutterstock, Inc.

Manufactured in the United States of America

East Peoria, IL/063692/300442

3 4 5 6 7 8 9 10 11   23 22 21 20 19 18 17 16

Table of Contents

What Is This Book?

Lutheranism 101 for Kids is a book to help you learn more about God's love for you in Christ and about your faith as a Christian. This book introduces you to three other books: the Bible, the Small Catechism by Martin Luther, and the hymnal *Lutheran Service Book*. In these pages, you'll find out how important each of these books can be for growing in faith.

So read on, grow, and learn!

Stuff You Need to Know

 From the Bible! Quotations from the Bible

 Believe, Teach, Confess! Quotations from creeds or Lutheran teachings

 Word Alert! Words and phrases quickly defined

Part 1: The Bible

1. Who Is God?

In this section, you'll learn about God and how we find out more about Him through

- nature and the things we experience;
- God's Word, the **Bible**; and
- God's characteristics, which show who He is and what He does.

How Do We Know God?

Maria shaped the clay into a blob, a bowl, and then a long-necked giraffe. She worked the clay in her hands until her fingers were orange and grubby. Then she sat back and looked at her giraffe. It was perfect.

As we hike up a mountain and see a waterfall, or view the huge Grand Canyon, we feel that someone must have made this. It's all so beautiful. This couldn't have happened by chance. Maria's clay did not become a giraffe by accident. The clay had to be dug out of the ground and put in a package, and then Maria had to shape it into something new. It took a **creator** to make it.

Pretend you are walking along the beach. You see the words "I love you" written in the sand. You don't know who wrote that message, but someone wrote it. It was not caused by waves, sun, or wind.

Now think about people and how complex we are. We are much more complicated than a message written in the sand. It seems Someone very wise has made us.

Creator: a person or thing who creates or makes something; God is the Creator of everything.

In the beginning, God created the heavens and the earth.
Genesis 1:1

Bible: Holy book that tells about God and what He has done for us; divided into two sections, the Old and New Testaments; also called **God's Word**.

Deep inside us, we also know the difference between right and wrong. We feel bad after telling a secret we promised not to share. People all over the world know that stealing and murder are wrong. Or we may feel good when we help someone in need. We are happy when we do the right thing and sad when we don't. Why is this?

God wrote the rules about how to live on our hearts. Even before we read the Bible, we know a little bit about what we are supposed to do and not do. We know that Someone is in charge of the universe because of what we see and feel. We want to learn more about this Someone. How can we know more?

What Does God Tell Us about Himself?

Riddle: What is black and white and read all over?
Answer: A book, of course!

We learned in the last section that God shows Himself in the world and in our hearts. But we need more knowledge, so God sent special messengers to bring **God's Word** to people. We call them prophets and apostles. Their message has been written and collected into a book called the Bible. This book is different from all others. It answers our questions about who God is. It tells us more about Him and about His **creation.**

An author writes the words in a book, so who is the author of the Bible? People wrote down the words of the Bible long ago, but God is the author. He worked through the writers to tell the message He wanted to share with us. We call this

inspiration. God inspired them to write the words about who He is and what He has done for us.

So what does God say to us in the Bible? The main message of the Bible is that God loves us through Jesus Christ. He is our heavenly Father, and He loves us as His dear children.

This message of God's love is told throughout the entire Bible. It is shown through the stories of God's people, from Adam to Noah to Ezekiel to Paul. The Bible is all about God's love for His people through their lives and stories. Jesus' love and kindness toward us is found all throughout the Bible.

The Bible is divided into two main parts: the **Old Testament** and the **New Testament**. The Old Testament begins with God's creation of the world: of light, water, carrots, jellyfish, tigers, and finally, the jewel of His creation, people. The Old Testament describes people and their stories—Noah and the flood; Moses and the parting of the Red Sea; Joseph and his beautiful coat; Daniel and the lions.

The Old Testament shows us God's love, but the New Testament gives us even more of the story.

The New Testament is about Jesus' birth, His ministry, and His miracles of healing the sick and raising the dead. The New Testament also describes the beginnings of the Church. But most important, it shows the saving work of Jesus, who suffered, died, and rose from the grave for us.

These two sections of the Bible are separated into sixty-six books, thirty-nine in the Old Testament, and twenty-seven in the New Testament.

Inspiration: God's work of leading the people to know the words to use when writing the Bible.

Old Testament: the first part of the Bible, which gives the history of God's people from creation through the time of the prophets.

New Testament: the second part of the Bible, which tells about Jesus, His work, and the Early Church.

Who Is God?
What Is He Like?

Holy Trinity:
term that refers to God as Father, Son, and Holy Spirit.

The Father is God, the Son is God, the Holy Spirit is God; and yet there are not three Gods, but one God. (The Athanasian Creed)

For his student-of-the-day presentation, Michael nervously walked to the front of the classroom. He cleared his throat. "I'm Michael Schmidt, but people call me Mike. I live with my mom and dad, my younger brother, who always bugs me, and two dogs. My favorite sports are soccer and basketball. My favorite food is chocolate cake."

When Michael told the class about himself, he told his name and some things that he enjoys, like sports and sweets. He's also the oldest child in his family.

In the same way, when we read the Bible, we find out more about God and what He's like. God is **Father**, **Son**, and **Holy Spirit**. He is the Father who made us; the Son, Jesus, who died to save us from our sins; and the Holy Spirit who gives us faith.

One term for God is the **Holy Trinity**. He is three persons and one God, three in one. A triangle is sometimes used as a symbol for God as the Holy Trinity. A triangle has three sides, but it's only one shape. This is similar to the concept of the Holy Trinity: three persons, but one God.

Knowing God's name gives us some information, but the Bible tells us much more. God is all powerful: He can do anything. God is always present: He is everywhere. He is not limited by space or time. God is all knowing: He knows everything that ever happened in the past and will ever happen in the present and future.

So God is mighty and powerful—and this could be a scary thing if we didn't know that God is also good and kind. He loves us and cares for us.

God is also **eternal**. He has always been and will always be. There never was a time when God did not exist. God never changes. People change, but God is always the same: kind and good.

As we discuss who God is, we also think about who we are. God is our Creator. We are His **creatures**. God made you to be who you are at this time, in this place. God, your Creator, loves you!

2. **What Is Sin?**

In this section, you'll learn more about

- how sin damaged our relationship with God;
- why bad things happen; and
- who's to blame for this mess.

What Does Sin Show about Our Relationship with God?

Chelsea and Shannon met at camp and became instant friends. They rode horses together, they gathered wood together, and they roasted marshmallows together. But Justine was jealous because she had signed up for camp with Shannon. Now Shannon was always off doing things with Chelsea. So Justine lied and told Chelsea that Shannon was making fun of her behind her back. It wasn't true, but Justine felt good—in a mean way—when she saw the hurt look on Shannon's face.

What messed up these friendships? **Sin**—the lying, the jealousy, and the anger. All of these things had hurt the girls. This is similar to our

For You formed my inward parts; You knitted me together in my mother's womb. I praise You, for I am fearfully and wonderfully made. Wonderful are Your works; my soul knows it very well. Psalm 139:13–14

Sin: a thought, word, or action against God's will.

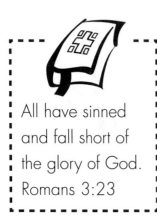

All have sinned
and fall short of
the glory of God.
Romans 3:23

relationship with God. Things were great until sin came into the world.

Adam and Eve had a perfect friendship with God in the Garden of Eden. Then the **devil** came along and tempted Eve to do something that God had told her not to do. She betrayed God; she sinned. Adam sinned too. This broke the friendship between God and Adam and Eve.

Sometimes we may think that sin isn't a big deal. Why do we have to live by so many rules, anyway? The truth is that God is in charge. We are His creatures and must live by His authority. God gave us the **Ten Commandments** to show us what we should do and what we should not do. But we don't follow the Commandments; we sin.

There are two types of sin: **original sin** and **actual sin**.

Original sin means we are sinful from our first moments within our mother's womb. Yes, even cute little babies are sinful. Sin affects all people, young and old. Actual sin describes all the things we do wrong—things we think, say, and do. Actual sin also refers to the times we are supposed to do good but don't.

Sin hurts us. It separates us from God. We are not in a close friendship with God because of sin. But there is Good News. The Good News is that Jesus saved us from our sin. God didn't simply tell us all of His rules and then leave us when we needed Him most. He gave us exactly what we need: He gave us Jesus.

Why Do Bad Things Happen, and Who's to Blame?

God created this world to be perfect. God, as the source of all that is good, makes only good things. He made a beautiful and perfect world for us because He loves us.

Then Satan and sin came along and messed up everything. Satan put a **temptation** in front of Eve in the Garden of Eden. A temptation is something that makes us want to sin.

For example, imagine that you are really hungry. You're at the grocery store, but you have no money. Then you see your favorite food—a chocolate bar. You want that chocolate bar, but without any money, you are tempted to steal it. The temptation itself is not sinful, but stealing is.

The same thing happened to Eve in the Garden of Eden. Satan told her to do something she wasn't supposed to do. That's the temptation. The problem is that she went ahead and did it. She sinned.

God's good creation was messed up by sin, and we're messed up because of sinfulness too. We get sicknesses like asthma and the flu. People get hurt and die every day. Poor people do not have enough food to eat. Tornadoes and floods destroy houses and neighborhoods.

Bad things happen as a result of sin, but these bad things were not part of God's creation. His creation was perfect and good. But when Satan and sin entered the world, things got messed up.

We sometimes add to our problems too. Pretend you went ahead and stole that chocolate bar from the grocery store. What would happen if you got caught? The grocery store manager might call the police. Your parents would get angry and punish

Temptation: anything that makes us want to sin.

11

The heart is deceitful above all things, and desperately sick; who can understand it? Jeremiah 17:9

you. They might not trust you as much anymore. All of these problems would have happened because of the sin you committed.

So who's to blame for the bad things that happen in the world? Who's to blame for all of the pain, sickness, sin, and death? God made a good and perfect world, a world without sin. But then sin and the devil came into the world. Sin is the devil's work.

However, God doesn't leave us alone in our sin. He helps us. God sent Jesus to save us from the mess we are in.

3. **Who Is Jesus?**

In this section, you'll learn more about how the Bible shows us who Jesus is. We'll learn that

- Jesus is human;
- Jesus is God;
- Jesus died to save us; and
- Jesus rose for us.

What Does the Bible Show Us about Jesus Being Human?

When Shawn saw his baby brother for the first time, he couldn't believe how tiny he was. He had ten little fingers and ten little toes. Shawn held his brother's hand. He looked into his brother's toothless mouth. He rubbed his bald head. His brother was a perfect, tiny person.

In Luke 2, we learn about Mary and Joseph and their journey to Bethlehem, where Jesus was born. Since there was no room for them in the inn, Jesus was placed in a manger for His bed. The shepherds came to worship Jesus after the angels sang "Glory to God in the highest!" You may have heard this story before, but have you ever really stopped to think about Jesus as a tiny, helpless baby, like Shawn's brother?

Jesus has existed forever; He is God, and as God, He is also eternal. But He wasn't always human. God chose a special time and place for Jesus to enter the world as a baby. God chose Mary as His mother, and God chose Joseph to care for them. And Jesus needed care. He was a baby. He cried, He dirtied diapers, and He ate and slept. He was a normal baby, except for one thing. Yes, Jesus was human, but He was also God. He was sinless and perfect.

Jesus grew up in a town called Nazareth. From what we know in the Bible, His life was not very different from anyone else's until He was an adult. Like us, Jesus had real temptations. The difference between Jesus and us is that Jesus never sinned. He did everything perfectly. He obeyed all of God's Laws without sinning a single time.

Jesus was fully human. He was born and grew up. He was hungry, thirsty, sad, and lonely. But while He went through all of our human experiences, He was also completely God at the same time.

And the Word became flesh and dwelt among us, and we have seen His glory, glory as of the only Son from the Father, full of grace and truth. John 1:14

Miracle: an action that only God has the power to do, like turning water into wine.

Forgiveness: showing mercy or kindness toward those who do wrong.

In [Christ] we have redemption through His blood, the forgiveness of our trespasses, according to the riches of [God's] grace. Ephesians 1:7

What Does the Bible Show Us about Jesus Being God?

We know that Jesus was human. He was born as a baby, He grew up in a family, and He experienced many of the same things we do. Jesus was also God. He showed this through the things that He knew and did. Jesus had the power to do things that only God can do. These are called **miracles**. One time, He turned water into wine. Another time, Jesus made a big storm stop. He also healed people who were sick and even made dead people come back to life.

Besides miracles, other things proved that Jesus was God. He knew things that no one else could have known. When He talked to the woman at the well (John 4), He knew all about her family and relationships even though He and she had never met before. He knew this because He is God—all knowing.

Jesus also did something special that proved He was God: He forgave sins. To **forgive** means to not hold someone's sins against him. Say your friend broke your bike because he was jealous and didn't want you to have it. Your friend sinned. Out of jealousy and meanness, he decided to take something away from you. If you were to forgive your friend, you would not hold this sin against him. You'd simply say, "I forgive you for the wrong you did to me."

Everyone makes mistakes, but there are plenty of times when we are feeling mad or upset, and we sin just because we feel like it. We know we are sinning, and we don't stop ourselves. We do it anyway. So we say we're

14

sorry for the wrong things we do—and we really mean it. We promise we'll try to not do those things again. And Jesus forgives us and forgets all about them. This is something only God can do, and it's one way that Jesus proves that He is God.

What Does the Bible Show Us through Jesus' death?

When you go to church, you see things that remind you about God and your belief in Him. You see an **altar**, or table, on which the bread and wine for Communion are spread. You see a **pulpit**, where the pastor stands to speak to us. You see a **baptismal font**, where babies and others are **baptized**. Another thing you see at Christian churches is a **cross**. Crosses come in all sizes, big and little. They can be made out of wood or metal. They can be fancy or simple. A cross helps us remember the most important thing Jesus did for us.

Jesus' most important work came at the end of His thirty-three years on the earth. We know that He did many miracles by calming the storms, healing the sick, and even raising people from the dead. But none of this was as important as what He did on the cross when He died for us.

It may seem strange to think that a person's death could be a good thing. It seems even stranger that the death of Jesus, God Himself, could be a good thing. But God sometimes surprises us. God often turns bad things into good things. This happens all throughout the Bible, but Jesus dying on the cross is the best example of God turning something bad into something good.

All through Jesus' life and ministry, He did good to help and teach people. Then the time came for

The reason the Son of God appeared was to destroy the works of the devil.
1 John 3:8b

"Behold, the Lamb of God, who takes away the sin of the world!"
John 1:29

Him to suffer, die, and rise from the dead. One Sunday, Jesus rode into the city of Jerusalem on a donkey. It was like a parade. People cheered for Jesus. Soon after this, however, things changed.

One night, Jesus had a special meal with His twelve **disciples**, or friends. One of the disciples, Judas, acted like he was Jesus' friend, but he was secretly working with the people who wanted to get rid of Jesus.

After the meal, while Jesus was praying, Judas led soldiers to Jesus. The soldiers arrested Him. They told lies about Him. They beat Him and hurt Him badly. Then they nailed Jesus to a cross to die.

While Jesus hung on the cross, the sun went dark for three hours, even though it was afternoon. There was an earthquake. These natural disasters showed that a terrible thing was happening—God Himself, the one who created life, was dying. But God sometimes surprises us. He takes bad things and makes them good. Although Jesus' death seemed like the most terrible thing that could have happened, it was actually something wonderful.

Someone had to be punished for the sin that came into the world. We should have been the ones who were punished for sin. It wasn't God's fault that we sinned. Even so, He took the punishment upon Himself. This is why we call Jesus our **Savior**. He saves us from our sins, which is a wonderful thing!

For God so loved the world, that He gave His only Son, that whoever believes in Him should not perish but have eternal life. John 3:16

Savior: a name for Jesus, who saves us from our sins.

What Does the Bible Show Us through Jesus' Resurrection?

When Jesus said "It is finished," it meant that He had done everything needed to take our sins away and bring us back to God. After that, Jesus took His last breath and died. Jesus' friends took His body to a grave. Instead of burying Jesus' body in the ground, a rich man let them use his grave, which was like a cave. They rolled a large stone in front of the cave to block the opening.

Jesus' body lay there in the cold, dark tomb. His friends could hardly believe it, but Jesus was really dead. This was why Jesus had to become human. He had to die so He could take our punishment for sin. But remember that Jesus is also God. Death couldn't hold Him!

Just after sunrise on the third day after Jesus died, some women came to Jesus' grave. They came to put spices on His body, as was the custom at that time. They arrived at the grave and expected to find the stone blocking the front of the cave. However, when they got there, they saw that the stone had been rolled away.

They entered the tomb, not understanding what had happened. There they saw an angel who said, "Do not be alarmed. You seek Jesus of Nazareth, who was crucified. He has risen; He is not here. See the place where they laid Him" (Mark 16:6). The women trembled in fear and astonishment. Jesus had risen from the dead!

Soon, Jesus' close friends also visited the tomb and found that Jesus was not there. This news was hard to believe, but then Jesus began appearing to His friends and talking with them. They could see

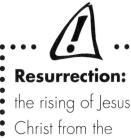

Resurrection: the rising of Jesus Christ from the dead.

[Jesus] was declared to be the Son of God in power according to the Spirit of holiness by His resurrection from the dead. Romans 1:4

He will wipe away every tear from their eyes, and death shall be no more, neither shall there be mourning, nor crying, nor pain anymore, for the former things have passed away. Revelation 21:4

the wounds in His body where the soldiers had hurt him. This helped them understand that He was the same Jesus they had known before. Jesus showed that He had truly come back to life.

Why was it important that Jesus rise from the dead? Jesus had to be human in order to die for sins. He was a man. He felt pain and hunger and got sleepy. He felt all of the same things that we do. Because of that, His body was weak and hurt when He was beaten. Then, after hanging on the cross, He died.

Jesus is also God, and as God, death couldn't hold Him. The **resurrection** shows us, beyond any doubt, that Jesus was God Himself. No person can make himself rise from the dead. Only God can do that. Jesus' resurrection also proves that God accepted Jesus' death to pay for our sins. Everything that was needed to take care of our problem with sin is finished.

4. **What Are Heaven and Hell?**

When Marcy got home from school, she found her mom crying in the kitchen. Marcy's stomach tightened in fear. She soon learned that her grandmother had died. Her family would be traveling to be with Grandpa and go to Grandma's funeral.

A couple of days later, when Marcy saw her Grandma in her casket, that fear in her stomach came back. Grandma was so quiet and still. She had had a giggly laugh and a quick smile before.

"Are you okay, Honey?" Mom asked, coming up next to her.

"Where's Grandma now?" Marcy asked. "Is she in heaven?"

When death touches our family or friends, we have serious questions. We not only wonder about whether our loved ones are in heaven or not, but we may have other questions too: "What is heaven like? What will happen to me when I die?"

We may not be able to answer every one of our questions about heaven until we get there. But the Bible does teach about heaven, and we know many wonderful things about it.

In **heaven**, we won't experience sin or sadness. There will be no tears, no pain, or sickness. There won't be cancer or hatred or bullying or even the common cold in heaven. There will be no skinned knees or bee stings or death. There will be only joy in Jesus. While all of the bad things will be gone, even more important is that we will be with Jesus. We will rejoice in our Savior and find perfect peace in Him.

The Bible teaches that **hell**, on the other hand, is a place of endless suffering and pain, where God's enemies are punished. Think of the things that upset us or make us sad: abused pets, sickness, or people without enough food. The worst things we experience, like car accidents or tornadoes or even strep throat, may seem awful.

But hell's suffering is much worse than any of these things. It's more

Heaven: life with God forever. **Hell:** separation from God forever.

painful and terrible than anything we can imagine. Sadly, this is the place where people go who do not believe in Jesus as their Savior, who reject God's Word and don't have faith in Him. This is why we must share the love of Jesus with everyone around us so they can know Him and go to heaven too.

As believers in Jesus, we can be certain of where we will go when we die. We can trust our Savior. In 2 Timothy 4:18, we read, "The Lord will rescue me from every evil deed and bring me safely into His heavenly kingdom." When someone asks us if we can be sure we'll go to heaven, we don't have to say, "I hope so." Rather, we say, "Yes, my Lord Jesus will take me there when I die."

So although we deal with difficult questions, like Marcy did when her grandma died, one of our questions about heaven can be answered. Will you, as a believer in Jesus, go there? Yes!

Part 2: The Small Catechism

Introduction

In the Bible, from the creation of the world to the resurrection of Jesus, we see how much God loves us. Sometimes we need help understanding these ideas, and that's where the **Catechism** comes in. Martin Luther wrote the Small Catechism almost five hundred years ago as a tool to help Christians, especially children, to understand the Bible. The Small Catechism helps us break down the teachings of the Bible in a clear way. This section is about the Catechism.

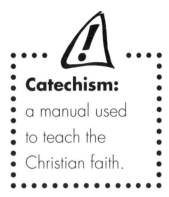

Catechism: a manual used to teach the Christian faith.

5. What Is Faith, and How Do We Get It?

In this section, you'll learn about

- what faith is; and
- how faith comes to us.

Now that we have learned about God and what He has done for us, we can turn to the idea of **faith**. Faith is trust or belief in something. Take the example of a chair. Think of your favorite chair. It may be old and worn out or brand new. But unless it's very old, you probably don't worry about it falling down when you sit on it, right?

Faith: belief in God.

Having faith in a chair to hold you is a little bit like having faith in God. We don't see or touch faith, but it's there, telling us that God loves us in Jesus. Through faith, we trust that the Bible is true, although we may not understand everything about it. We have faith in our Father, who made us and loves us; in Jesus, who died to save us; and in the Holy Spirit, who helps us grow in our faith. We believe!

In the previous section of this book, we learned about Jesus' work of saving us from our sins. We learned about how He suffered, died, and then rose from the dead. All of this was amazing, life-giving work. However, unless we believe through faith that this saving work was done for us, we can't enjoy the benefits of it. We can hold onto these beliefs because we have faith. Faith takes what Jesus did and says "Yes, I believe that this is what Jesus did for me."

Faith isn't something we have by ourselves. God the Holy Spirit gives us faith. Faith is a gift of God that helps us grow in our knowledge of Him and believe in Him. Ephesians 2:8–9 says, "For by grace you have been saved through faith. And this is not your own doing; it is the gift of God, not a result of works, so that no one may boast."

Notice what this verse says: that faith is not "your own doing." It doesn't come from ourselves, but as a gift from God. This is more good news, added to what God has already done for us: not only did Jesus take on our punishment for sin and promise to take believers to heaven, but God also gives us the faith to believe in Him and His promise. What great news!

6. What Is the Church?

Kaylie folded her hands and began the poem: "Here is the church. . . ."

She put her two pointer fingers together. "Here is the steeple. Open it up. . . ." She turned her hands over and wiggled her fingers. "And here's all the people!"

When you hear the word **church**, what do you think of? Sometimes the first thing we think of is the building where we come together on Sunday morning. When we say we "go to church," we usually mean that we go to our church building. So what does the Bible say about the word *church*?

It may be helpful to know that the Church is not only a building. Church buildings show us that God's house is special. We set aside a place to pray, listen to God's Word, sing, and receive God's gift of forgiveness. The cross, altar, and pulpit help us to think about what God has done for us. The designs in the stained glass windows can help us learn Bible stories. But the building itself, while special, isn't why the church exists.

Also, the Church is not a club, like Boy Scouts or Girl Scouts. People who like the same things join clubs to enjoy activities together. While we have things in common with other Christians and do many things together, that is not the main reason for the Church.

What makes the Church different? Jesus. He is with us as we gather for the Divine Service. We receive gifts from God. He speaks to us through the Bible readings and preaching. God saves us in Baptism by taking away our sins. God forgives us through His body and blood in Holy Communion. In church, God makes our faith grow.

[Jesus said:] "For where two or three are gathered in My name, there am I among them." Matthew 18:20

Church: community of believers in Christ who come together to receive God's gifts.

May you be strengthened with all power, according to His glorious might . . . giving thanks to the Father, who has qualified you to share in the inheritance of the saints in light. Colossians 1:11–12

In the Bible, Jesus tells us that the Church is like a body. Think of a human body, with a head, arms, legs, fingers, and everything else. If we compare the Church to a body, Jesus is the head. He leads us; He is in charge. We are His hands and feet, who do loving things for others.

Yes, the Church is much more than a building. It's also much more than a club. The Church is a community of believers in Christ who come together to receive God's gifts. It's all about God giving Himself to us.

What Are Saints?

A father and his son visited a large church with stained glass windows. They looked at the pictures in the windows, which showed different saints and how they served Jesus.

The father asked his son, "Do you know who the saints were?"

"Sure," said the boy. "The saints are the people that the sun shines through."

A **saint** is someone, on earth now or in heaven, through whom God the Son, Jesus, shines. Many people think that a saint is a super-holy Christian who never does anything wrong. However, that is not how the word is used in the Bible. Saints are all those who follow Jesus Christ and live by His teachings. Saints are not only the special people who do amazing things. Saints are regular Christians who are saved by Jesus and follow Him.

Saint: a believer in Jesus Christ, baptized and filled with His Spirit, who lives by His teaching.

Sometimes you'll hear people say, "Well, I'm no saint." What they mean is "I'm not perfect," or "I make mistakes." Saints—Christians—are not perfect people. We are sinners and saints at the same time. That doesn't mean we can sin and do

What about Angels?

Are angels little babies with wings? Are angels people who died and now are in heaven? From what the Bible tells us, the answer is no. Angels are different creatures than people. You are not able to turn into a different creature, either now or after you die. God made you and every person as His prized creation. He made angels different from people.

Angels are more like soldiers than cuddly babies. They are strong and mighty. God sends angels to bring messages to people. When Mary found out she would be the mother of Jesus, it was an angel that told her the news.

Angels can be scary too. When they speak to people, the first thing they often say is "Don't be afraid!" (see Luke 1:30; 2:9–10).

Angels are a different creation, like you are different from a lion or a polar bear. And this is just the way God wants it!

whatever we want. Instead, as believers in Jesus, we want to do what He wants for us.

We're not saints because of the good things we do. We're saints, here and now, because we are baptized into Christ and forgiven because of His death on the cross.

7. **What Is Baptism?**

In this section, you'll learn

- what is needed for Baptism; and

- what the benefits of Baptism are.

Timothy peered over the edge of the baptismal font. His mom, dad, aunt, and uncle stood with him in the front of the church. Timothy's baby sister, Erin, was being baptized. Aunt Jenny gently held Erin over the water. Pastor Williams used a seashell to pour water over her tiny head.

He said, "Erin, I baptize you in the name of the Father . . ." *splash!* "and of the Son . . ." *splash!* "and of the Holy Spirit" *splash!*

As Timothy watched, he felt a splash of water land on his nose.

Timothy, at four years old, did not completely understand everything that happened at his sister's Baptism. He knew the water was regular wet water. He'd felt it on his nose. But he knew that something about Baptism made this different from any other bath.

What Is Needed for Baptism?

In the Church, we use the word *Baptism* to talk about this special washing. In Baptism, there must be two things:

1. water; and
2. the name of God in Three Persons—Father, Son, and Holy Spirit.

The water used in Baptism is not magic water. When you wash your face, brush your teeth, or get a drink, you turn on the faucet and out comes clean water. Water for Baptism also comes from a faucet in the church.

It's when that plain water is combined with God's Word that something special happens. God uses this water to give a gift of forgiveness to the baptized. He uses everyday things like water to share His gifts with us. In Baptism, the pastor pours water on the person being baptized, and this water, along with God's Word, is what Baptism is. The water by itself is ordinary water, but when it is combined with God's Word, it gives us life, forgiveness, and new birth in the Holy Spirit.

The second thing needed for Baptism is God's name. After Jesus rose from the dead, He gave His followers instructions about how to help people believe in God. He said, "Go therefore and make disciples of all nations, baptizing them in the name of the Father and of the Son and of the Holy Spirit" (Matthew 28:19). Jesus Himself told His followers to do this, to baptize in God's name.

Baptism is a sacrament. In sacraments, God gives us forgiveness through a physical element, like water, combined with His

Baptism: a sacrament, or Means of Grace, in which God bestows grace and forgiveness upon the baptized with water and in the name of the Father, Son, and Holy Spirit.

Sacrament: a sacred act that (1) was instituted by God, (2) has a visible element, and (3) offers the forgiveness of sins earned by Christ. (From *Lutheranism 101*)

Font: the bowl or container to hold the water for Baptism.

Word. Baptism and the Lord's Supper are both Sacraments. During a Baptism, the name of God is spoken, the water is poured, and a new child of God is born!

Usually, Baptism takes place in church at a baptismal font. A font is a container that holds the water for Baptism. Fonts are often carved out of wood or marble, with a metal bowl that sits inside. With the pastor, the family of the baptized person stands at the font and speaks for the child if needed.

We often see babies being baptized in church, like Timothy's sister, Erin. Many parents choose to have their babies baptized soon after they are born. Why do we baptize babies? It's because we are all born into sin, so even babies are sinful.

Jesus got mad at His followers when they tried to push away the children from seeing Him. Jesus said, "Let the children come to Me; do not hinder them, for to such belongs the kingdom of God'" (Mark 10:14). However, people of any age, from tiny babies to children to adults, may be baptized. God's gifts are available to everyone, so Baptism is a gift for all.

What Are the Benefits of Baptism?

The gift of Baptism is God's saving love poured out for us. Through it, God forgives our sins. Sin is like the stickiest, stinkiest, slimiest mess. We need a bath to clean up this mess. God's bath in Baptism washes away these sins. No sin is too strong, too grimy, or too dirty for God to clean up. God washes the sinful person until he is sparkling, clean, and bright white.

In Baptism, God also rescues us from death and the devil. Think of the word *rescue*. Firefighters rescue those who are stuck inside burning buildings. The Coast Guard rescues those who are lost at sea. These people cannot save themselves. They need someone to save them. That's what God does through Baptism. On our own, we can't get away from sin, death, or the devil. But God rescues us, taking our sin away and freeing us from the devil.

In Baptism, God also gives us eternal life. We can exercise and eat healthy foods so we can live longer and healthier, but everyone dies eventually. However, that is not the end for Christians. When Jesus returns to the earth, He will call all believers, living and dead. We will rise to meet our Savior, Jesus, and live with Him forever in heaven.

We are saints and sinners at the same time. Our Baptism makes us saints: holy ones whom God loves and cherishes. But we still sin in our thoughts, words, and actions. So, every day, it's important for us to remember our Baptism, repent of our sins, and believe that Jesus died for those sins. We thank God for washing away our sins in Baptism because of Jesus' death for us. Enjoy your bath!

Baptism . . . now saves you.
1 Peter 3:21

Whoever believes and is baptized will be saved.
Mark 16:16

8. **What Is Confession?**

Lindsay stood in the principal's office. Her hands were shaking.

"I'll ask you again," the principal, Mr. Frost, said. "Did you hit Mary?"

"No," Lindsay said. *Okay*, she thought, *that's a bit of a lie, but it wasn't my fault!*

Confession: saying our sinful thoughts, words, and actions.
Absolution: the pastor's announcement, with Christ's authority, that we are truly and completely forgiven.

[Jesus said:] "If you forgive the sins of any, they are forgiven them; if you withhold forgiveness from any, it is withheld."
John 20:23

"Several people *saw* you hit Mary," Mr. Frost said. "What happened?"

Lindsay blurted out, "It wasn't my fault! She is always being a bully, shoving people around! She never gets in trouble! It's not fair!"

Mr. Frost tilted his head. "And . . ."

"Yes, I hit her," Lindsay finally admitted.

It's hard to confess that we have done something wrong. We have to say that we messed up; being unwilling to admit our faults is wrong. Confessing, or saying that we did wrong, is important for Christians. We also trust that along with confession, we'll be forgiven.

Confession has two parts. The first part is **confessing** your sins, which means you admit the sins you have committed. The second part, **absolution**, is when the pastor tells you by Christ's authority that you are completely forgiven.

Confessing our sins is more than saying what we have done wrong. Confession includes **repentance**. Repentance means that you are sorry for your sin, you want to be forgiven, and you really do not want to do that sin again. Don't confess something that you are not sorry for but don't plan on stopping. Instead, think about the Ten Commandments. Ask yourself if you have kept them perfectly in thought, word, and action.

Keep in mind that real guilt is different from a feeling. A bank robber is guilty whether or not he feels bad about his actions. And a kid who feels bad because she had the flu and missed church is not guilty, no matter what her feelings are. She has not sinned. God's Word tells us what is sinful and what isn't; that's why we need to read it.

In church, we have Confession at the beginning of our worship service. The whole congregation gives them absolution, telling everyone that for Jesus' sake they are forgiven.

Privately confessing our sins to our pastor can also be good. When the pastor tells us we are forgiven for the sake of Christ, it is as if we hear it from the mouth of God Himself.

9. What Is the Lord's Supper?

In this section, you'll learn about the Lord's Supper. You'll learn

- what is needed for the Lord's Supper; and
- what the benefits of the Lord's Supper are.

One day, a farmer went out to plant a field. In Jesus' day, farmers used their hands to sow handfuls of tiny seeds over a field. As the farmer scattered the seed over the soil, some of it fell on a hard, worn path nearby. Some landed in rocks at the field's edge. Some seed landed in soil that was full of thistles. And some of the seed landed in the dark, rich, weed-free dirt. The seed was scattered everywhere, but it didn't grow everywhere.

You may recognize this parable that Jesus told about God's Word being scattered and growing into faith (Luke 8:4–8, 11–15). Jesus says that the seed is like God's Word, which is spread far and wide. Some people hear God's Word, but they don't believe it because the devil snatches it away. Some believe for a little while, but then they stop believing because they are too worried about life. Others, the good soil, receive God's Word, hold it in their hearts, and show God's Word in their lives.

Like the seed, God's Word is first planted in our hearts in Baptism. We must continue to grow in God's Word and in faith. God feeds us each Sunday as we hear His Word explained in the pastor's sermon. We are also fed by the **Lord's Supper.** Jesus' body and blood strengthen and help us to grow in faith.

The Lord's Supper can be called **"Holy Communion,"** "the Sacrament of the Altar," or "the Eucharist." All of these terms refer to God's gift of forgiveness through the body and blood of Christ, given to believers. It is a sacrament, like Baptism, in which God gives us His grace through physical things. Jesus Himself began the Lord's Supper on the night before He was crucified. He said what we call "the Words of Institution," which pastors still say today.

In church, when we celebrate the Lord's Supper, the wine and bread are prepared and set on the altar before the service. Then, shortly after the sermon is given, the pastor recites the Words of Institution:

Our Lord Jesus Christ, on the night when He was betrayed, took bread, and when He had given thanks, He broke it and gave it to the disciples and said: "Take, eat; this is My body, which is given for you. This do in remembrance of Me."

In the same way also He took the cup after supper, and when He had given thanks, He gave it to them, saying: "Drink of it, all of you; this cup is the new testament in My blood, which is shed for you for the forgiveness of sins. This do, as often as you drink it, in remembrance of Me." (*LSB*, pp. 162, 179, 197, 209, 217; adapted from Matthew 26:26–28; Mark 14:22–24; Luke 22:19–20; 1 Corinthians 11:23–25)

These are not magical words. But we use them because Jesus said them when He gave His body and blood to His disciples at their Last Supper. We don't understand exactly how bread and wine can become Jesus' body and blood. We know that in the Lord's Supper, we receive this amazing gift from Jesus for our forgiveness. Our faith, like the seeds in Jesus' parable, grows as we receive God's gifts of grace in His Word, in Baptism, and in the Lord's Supper.

What Are the Benefits of the Lord's Supper?

Many blessings come to us from the Lord's Supper. As in Baptism, God uses everyday things, like bread and wine, to show us His love. In the Lord's Supper, through bread and wine, God forgives us with Jesus' own body and blood. We can trust that Jesus forgives us and removes our sins because of His death on the cross.

Two of the most meaningful words in the Bible are the words "for you." On the night before Jesus was crucified, He took bread and wine and said that these were His body and blood. His body, He said, was "given for you" (Luke 22:19), and His blood was "poured out for you"(v. 20), so that our sins would be forgiven. Notice that Jesus says He is given "for you." These words show that everything Jesus did, He did for you.

With Baptism and the Lord's Supper, we can see, feel, and taste the mercy of God. We can slosh in the waters of Baptism. We can taste the bread and wine of the Lord's Supper in our mouths. God uses these ordinary, regular things to give us His gifts.

When we come to the Lord's Supper, we come with humility. Because of our sin, we do not deserve God's mercy. But we trust that He will forgive us, so we come with repentance to receive His gifts.

We must be careful with the Lord's Supper and not treat it like a joke or something unimportant. God tells us that we must be careful with this gift. After all, it is Jesus' body and blood poured out for us. This is why Lutheran churches wait to give the Lord's Supper to people until they have learned more about their faith and about Jesus.

[Jesus said:] "If you then, who are evil, know how to give good gifts to your children, how much more will your Father who is in heaven give good things to those who ask Him!"
Matthew 7:11

During instruction, students learn about the whole story of salvation—about the Ten Commandments, the Creeds, the Lord's Prayer, Baptism, the Lord's Supper, and Confession. To prepare for going to the Lord's Supper, we must repent of our sins, believe that Jesus has paid for them in full, and trust that we are receiving His body and blood in the Sacrament. When we eat and drink in repentance and with faith, the blessings of Christ's sacrifice become ours.

10. **What Is Prayer?**

Prayer is, very simply, talking to God. We can talk to God wherever we are. We can give Him thanks when we receive our food at lunchtime. We can ask for help and strength when we are sick in bed. We can say we're sorry to God when we do something wrong. We can pray alone or with a group of other Christians.

Jesus taught us a prayer that helps to guide our words as we pray. We call this the Lord's Prayer. The Lord's Prayer teaches us to come to God and not be nervous about talking to Him. God wants to answer our prayers, just like a loving father wants to give his children the best. Loving fathers know how to give children good gifts. Think of how much more God, our loving heavenly Father, wants to hear and bless us! So we should talk to Him every day.

When we pray, we ask God to do what He wants for us. So we don't pray for things that we know would be against what He wants. We shouldn't pray, for example, that bad things would happen to people who have hurt us. Instead, we

The Lord's Prayer

Our Father who art in heaven, hallowed be Thy name, Thy kingdom come, Thy will be done on earth as it is in heaven. Give us this day our daily bread; and forgive us our trespasses as we forgive those who trespass against us; and lead us not into temptation, but deliver us from evil. For Thine is the kingdom and the power and the glory forever and ever. Amen.

should pray that God would help us to love our enemies. We shouldn't pray that we get everything we want. Instead, we should pray that God would make our faith stronger to accept whatever happens. God promises to hear our prayers for the sake of Jesus, but that does not mean that we can pray for things that are against what God wants.

God answers our prayers in different ways. He can say yes, and we receive what we ask for. He can say no, and we pray for the strength to be content with what we have. Or He can say, "I have a better idea." This means we may not always get exactly what we want, and that we need to be open to His will—in other words, to whatever God has in mind for us.

Let's say you really want a new bicycle, so you pray for it. In the Bible, God has not promised that everyone will get new bicycles, so we don't know that this is God's will. We know that He wants to provide for His children, though, so you can ask. God's answer may come in different ways. Maybe He'll bless you by providing for you through your parents. Maybe He'll help you to earn money and save up for a new bike. Or maybe you won't get that bike you want.

God wants us to learn to trust in Him as our loving Father, no matter what happens in our lives.

11. **Who Are Pastors?**

There's a familiar joke about pastors which says that they work only one day a week—Sunday. That would be an easy job, wouldn't it? However, being a pastor is much more than just showing up on Sunday morning. So what does a pastor do all day?

The most important work of the **pastor** is sharing God's Word with people. He does this in different ways, and the most important way is leading the congregation's Sunday worship. When a pastor speaks to people during worship, he gives a **sermon**, a talk about the Bible reading for that day. In his sermon, the pastor will talk about following God's Law, or rules. But he talks most of all about God's love for us and how Jesus died on the cross to pay for our sins. Pastors spend many hours each week reading and writing and praying about what they will say in the sermon.

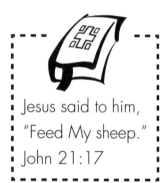

Jesus said to him, "Feed My sheep." John 21:17

The pastor also shows God's love to the people in the church by giving them Jesus' body and blood in Communion. He performs Baptisms in order to share God's gift of eternal life. He hears people confess their sins and tells them that God forgives them. He shares God's Word at funerals with the families of those who have died. Performing weddings is also part of a pastor's duties.

The pastor often teaches Bible classes, new member classes, and confirmation classes. He must take time to get ready to teach all of these classes.

The pastor is also the leader in prayer. He prays for the needs of the people in the church, the community, and the world. He prays with people who are sick or who need someone to help them remember to trust in God.

He visits those who are in the hospital or who cannot come to church. He works with kids and explains God's Word to them. He also cares for the elderly who are at the end of their lives.

The pastor works hard to spread the message about Christ to all people. He is like a delivery person who delivers flowers. He delivers the gift, but it's not from him. It's from God. The pastor brings us God's Word in preaching sermons, in giving Jesus' body and blood in Communion, in administering Baptism, and in pronouncing the Absolution.

The pastor is a regular guy. He may be big or short or gray-haired. He may like football or yard work or movies. He's a regular person, like you, but he has special gifts to give us, gifts from God Himself.

One last question that comes up is about a pastor's "uniform." Many Lutheran pastors wear special robes during church services. They also often wear black shirts with white collars. These clothes set them apart from everyone else, but not because of something special in them. These clothes remind us that pastors deliver God's gifts. They bring us Jesus!

12. **Who Is Martin Luther?**

This book is all about what **Lutherans** believe, but you may be wondering what "Lutheran" means. The word *Lutheran* comes from the name of a pastor who lived in Germany in the 1500s. His name was **Martin Luther,** and he was a teacher, pastor, writer, husband, and father.

At the time when Martin Luther lived, the Church was very different. The worship services and Bible readings were in Latin, and few people understood that language. Luther wanted everyone to be able to understand what they were hearing so they could learn and understand God's Word.

Also, many people were confused about what happened when their loved ones died. They thought it was necessary to pay money to help them get to heaven. Luther helped people understand that this was not what the Bible taught.

The main things Luther did were teach, preach, and write about Jesus saving us from our sins. Luther wanted to make sure that message was the main thing people heard when they came to church.

When he was a younger man, Luther often became worried about the sins he had committed. He tried to think of everything he'd ever done wrong so he could ask for forgiveness. He knew that sin made God angry. Luther didn't clearly understand that because of Jesus' sacrifice for sin, God was no longer angry. Then he learned from God's Word that Jesus had taken the punishment of sin for us. He was free because of Jesus! He was forgiven!

> For I am not ashamed of the gospel, for it is the power of God for salvation to everyone who believes. . . . For in it the righteousness of God is revealed from faith for faith, as it is written, "The righteous shall live by faith." Romans 1:16–17

Martin Luther realized that everyone needed to hear this message. Everyone needed to know that for Jesus' sake, God loves us. Martin Luther wanted to keep Jesus and His love for us as the most important thing that was explained and taught at church.

As Luther began to understand the Bible better, he started teaching others. They gathered and worshiped together. They heard God's Word and the church service in their own language. They heard sermons that clearly showed God's love in Christ.

This time in history is called "the Reformation." To *reform* means to "make changes in something in order to improve it." That was what Martin Luther hoped to do—to reform the Church, not create a new church. The people who returned to the teachings of the Bible called themselves Lutherans.

Through the years, the Lutheran Church has changed and grown. The reforms of Martin Luther helped to shape the Church today. We teach Christ crucified, our Savior from sin. It's great to be a Lutheran!

Part 3: The Hymnal

Hymn: a song of praise to God.

Hymnal: a collection of hymns.

Liturgy: the order of the hymns, prayers, and other parts of the Divine Service.

So far, we've discussed two books: the Bible and the Small Catechism. Now we turn to one other book, the **hymnal**. The hymnal is filled with songs of praise to God, or **hymns**. Also included in the hymnal is our **liturgy**. Liturgy gives us the order to our worship services. We may begin with a hymn, continue with a Bible reading, go on to the sermon, and finish with the Lord's Supper. The hymns, liturgy, and much more are included in a hymnal. The current hymnal for the Lutheran Church— Missouri Synod is called the *Lutheran Service Book (LSB)*.

In this section, you'll explore

- what hymns are; and
- what we can learn from them.

13. **What Are Hymns?**

Imagine it: the Israelites had been slaves in Egypt for many years. Finally, God set them free, but Pharaoh, Egypt's king, sent soldiers after them to bring them back. And then they got stuck. The Red Sea was in front of them, and Pharaoh's army was behind them. They were cornered.

So God made a way for His people. At a time when they could not see a way out, God parted the Red Sea so the Israelites could escape. God held back the waters, and His people were free.

On that day, songs of praise filled the mouths of those whom God had rescued. Moses' sister, Miriam, sang: "Sing to the LORD, for He has triumphed gloriously; the horse and his rider He has thrown into the sea" (Exodus 15:21). We still sing words of praise today, like Miriam and Moses did thousands of years ago.

Hymns that are God's Word set to music are **canticles**. One of these canticles is the "Song of Moses and Israel" (*LSB* 925) from the Book of Exodus in the Old Testament. Another canticle is Mary's song, the "Magnificat," from Luke 1:46–55 (*LSB*, p. 231). Other hymns were written by poets and musicians who read God's Word and then wrote words and music based on it.

In Christian hymns, the most important thing is the words. The finest hymns focus on Jesus Christ, who He is and what He has done for us. A hymn may help us to say we're sorry for our sins, or help us to sing a song of praise when we are filled with joy, or help to cheer us up when we are down.

Since music often is a great tool for memorization, learning hymns can help us to remember God's Word. Think about the ABCs. How did you learn them? By singing a song. So, by singing hymns, we can learn and remember God's Word. When we consider God and His loving kindness, we can't help but sing!

What Can We Learn from Hymns?

For each hymn in the hymnal, information is given about that hymn's tune, text, and meter. Look at the song "Jesus Loves Me" (*LSB* 588) on page 45. At the top of the page are three pieces of information. At the top right corner is the name of the section in the hymnal. This hymn is in "The Word of God" section. Some sections are named after seasons in the Church Year, so, at the top of the page, you might see "Christmas" or "Pentecost." Other sections show categories, like "Communion" or "Prayer." Also at the top of the page are the title of the hymn ("Jesus Loves Me") and the hymn number (588).

Most of the page is filled with the music for the hymn. "Jesus Loves Me" has four systems. Reading the words and music in a hymn is different from reading a book. For the first stanza, you read the top line of words in each line of music. After the first system, you skip down to the second, third, and other systems to continue the first stanza. After stanza 1, you go back to the top and read the second line of words in each system of music.

If a hymn is long, the last stanzas may be written below the music, like little paragraphs. Sometimes the same words will be shown in another language.

At the bottom of the page is more information about the hymn. The name of the tune is in the bottom right-hand corner. Tunes may be used for more than one hymn. (In this case, the name of the tune is the same as the hymn title.)

Next, you'll find the meter of the hymn. For "Jesus Loves Me," it's "7 7 7 7 and refrain." This shows the number of syllables for each verse of the hymn. Think of it as a poem. Certain types of poems, like haiku, have a certain number of syllables per line. This breakdown is similar to the meter of a hymn.

Also at the bottom of the page are the names of the people who wrote the tune and the words of the hymn. There also may be a Bible verse, which shows where the idea or words of the hymn came from.

THE WORD OF GOD • Title

Jesus Loves Me

588 • Season of the Church Year or category

• Hymn number

• Verse

• System

1 Je - sus loves me! This I know, For the Bi - ble tells me so.
2 Je - sus loves me! He who died Heav-en's gates to o - pen wide.

Lit - tle ones to Him be-long; They are weak, but He is strong.
He has washed a - way my sin, Lets His lit - tle child come in.

Refrain

Yes, Je - sus loves me! Yes, Je - sus loves me!

Yes, Je - sus loves me! The Bi - ble tells me so.

1 Cristo me ama, bien lo sé;
  su Palabra me hace ver
  que los niños son de aquel
  quien es nuestro amigo fiel.

2 Cristo me ama, me salvó,
  en la cruz por mí murió;
  mi pecado perdonó;
  vida eterna me donó.

Estribillo   Sí, Cristo me ama; sí, Cristo me ama;
              sí, Cristo me ama; la Biblia dice así.

• Tune name
• Meter
• Bible verses that words may have come from

Text : Anna B. Warner, 1820–1915 alt.; Spanish tr. unknown
Music: William B. Bradbury, 1816–68

Text and music: Public domain

JESUS LOVES ME
77 77 and refrain

Matt. 19:14; Titus 3:9; Eph. 3:17b–19

14. **What Is a Creed? What Do I Believe?**

A **creed** is a statement about what a person believes. The Christian Church has three creeds, or statements of belief, that tell basic Christian teachings about who God is and what He has done for us. These are the Apostles' Creed, the Nicene Creed, and the Athanasian Creed.

The first creed, the Apostles' Creed is the oldest, shortest, and most basic. It wasn't written by the apostles, but it is based on their teaching and preaching.

In this creed, we state our common beliefs in the Father, the Son, and the Holy Spirit. We begin by saying we believe that the Father is our Creator who made us and loves us. Next, we describe what we believe about Jesus and His saving work on the cross for us. We tell about Jesus suffering, dying, and rising again for us. Finally, we declare our belief in the Holy Spirit, the Christian Church, and eternal life.

Another creed of the Church is the Nicene Creed. We usually speak this creed during a Communion service. In the Nicene Creed, there is more detail about our belief in Jesus. It was written at a time when people were confused about who Jesus was. Was He God? Was He a man? How could He be both God and man at the same time? These were some of the questions people were asking. The Nicene Creed helps to answer those questions.

The last creed of the Church is the Athanasian Creed, which is the longest of the three. In the Athanasian Creed, like the others, we confess our belief in God as Father, Son, and Holy Spirit. This

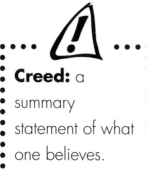

Creed: a summary statement of what one believes.

creed, which we usually say together on Trinity Sunday in the early summer, gives more detail about who God is as the Trinity, Three in One.

With our words, we boldly and joyfully say, "This is what I believe." We also are saying that yes, we believe what Christians have believed for hundreds of years.

In the Book of Mark, we read about a father who brought his son to Jesus for healing. The boy had an unclean spirit, and he needed Jesus to cast the demon out of him. Jesus told the father to trust in Him and believe. The father responded, "I believe; help my unbelief!" (Mark 9:24). We may feel this way sometimes too. We may have questions or doubts about God or our faith in Him, and we can also say boldly and freely to Jesus: "I believe; help my unbelief!"

15. What Is the Church Year?

For Andrew's birthday, he invited his friends to cosmic bowling. They ate pizza, bowled, and played arcade games. He received the remote control helicopter he'd hoped for. His birthday party was great, and Andrew was disappointed when it was over.

But Thanksgiving and Christmas were coming soon. Then they would celebrate the New Year, and Easter, and on around the calendar Andrew would go. In time, Andrew would have another birthday.

The Christian Year

The Church Year

Advent · Christmas · Epiphany · Lent · Easter · Season after Pentecost (Trinity)

Our lives, like Andrew's, are similar to a wheel—each year goes around and around as we move forward throughout the years. Along the way, we experience special times, like birthdays, holidays, and seasons.

The Church has a calendar like this too. We call it the **Church Year**, and it has special days and seasons. Each of these days and seasons gives us a reason to celebrate God's work for us.

The Time of Christmas

Advent

The Church Year begins with the season of Advent, four Sundays before Christmas. The word *advent* means "coming," and in this season, we prepare for the coming of Jesus on Christmas. We also prepare our hearts for Jesus' return at the end of time. We must be ready for His coming. Because we want to live in heaven with Him, we hope that every day could be the day Jesus returns. We are sorry for our sins, and we receive God's gift of forgiveness with joy.

The cloths on the altar in Advent are a deeper color of blue or violet. Blue is the color of hope, and we are filled with hope as we expect Jesus' return; violet is the color for repentance. We pray, "Come, Lord Jesus!"

Your church may have an Advent wreath with four candles, three blue or violet and one pink. The pink candle stands for joy. There may also be a white Christ candle in the center. A candle is lit for each week of Advent.

Christmas

On December 25, we celebrate Jesus' birth. In our churches, we usually celebrate on Christmas Eve and Christmas Day, but the Church Year season of Christmas actually lasts for a total of twelve days.

At Christmastime, churches are decorated with Christmas trees, candles, and lights. The altar is covered in white. White is usually the color of joy or purity, so it shows our joy in Jesus and His holiness and innocence. The reason for Christmas is to celebrate the birth of Christ. Jesus became a baby at a particular time and place. He became *Immanuel*—"God with us."

Epiphany

Next is the season of Epiphany (pronounced ee-PI-fan-ee). This season lasts six to eight weeks, depending on the date of Easter. During Epiphany, we remember that Jesus came for everyone in the world. On the first Sunday of Epiphany, we read about the Magi, or Wise Men, who traveled great distances to bring gifts to Jesus (Matthew 2:1–10). These people were from a different land. They followed a star to find the new King, Jesus, and they gave Him their gifts of gold, frankincense, and myrrh.

The colors of Epiphany are white for the first two Sundays, and then green. The color green shows that God is making the Church grow as the message of Jesus' love is being spread all over the world.

Lent

The next season is **Lent,** which begins forty days before Easter. The first day of Lent is Ash Wednesday. In Ash Wednesday services in many churches, the pastor uses ashes to draw a cross on people's foreheads. What is the purpose of this? Answering that question helps us to understand the reason for the season of Lent. During Lent, we are sorry for our sin and the things we have done wrong. Our sins are so serious that the punishment is death and eternal separation from God, but Jesus took this punishment upon Himself. So we repent, asking Jesus to help us be humble and admit our sin. The color of Lent is purple, for repentance.

At the end of Lent, the week before Easter, we observe **Holy Week**. It starts with Palm Sunday, when we hear the Bible story of Jesus entering Jerusalem on a donkey. People waved palm branches and shouted, "Hosanna to the Son of David!" (Matthew 21:9). In this way, the people showed their love and respect for Jesus as their king. He truly is our King who won the victory over sin, death, and the devil. Jesus showed His humility by riding on a donkey. His work was not yet completed. He would still have to die.

Holy Week continues with **Holy Thursday**, which is also called Maundy Thursday. On this day, Jesus gave the Lord's Supper for the first time. The disciples gathered to eat together; Jesus knew it would be their last meal with Him before He was crucified. At this meal, Jesus gave them bread and wine, saying, "This is My body. . . . This is My blood" (Matthew 26:26, 28).

Good Friday is the day that changed the world. This is the day Jesus made everything right between God and people. He took the punishment for all the sins of all the world, but doing so cost Jesus His human life. Right before Jesus died, He cried out, "It is finished" (John 19:30). Everything was done: Jesus had died for our sin; He had brought us back to God.

The Time of Easter

Easter

Our sadness about Jesus' death on Good Friday ends as we celebrate His resurrection on Easter. We decorate the church with Easter lilies and white cloths on the altar to show our great joy in Jesus and our new life in Him. We sing "Alleluia!" as praise fills our hearts. Jesus has risen! He has risen indeed! Alleluia!

The season of Easter lasts for forty days, until we celebrate Jesus' ascension, when He went up into heaven (Luke 24:50–53). Jesus would no longer be on the earth in human form, but He is with us in Baptism, in the Lord's Supper, and in God's Word.

The Time of the Church

Pentecost

Ten days after Ascension Day comes Pentecost. On the Day of Pentecost, we read about the Holy Spirit resting on the disciples like tongues of fire (Acts 2:1–21). This image of the Spirit as fire is the reason we drape our altars with red. The Holy Spirit filled the disciples with strength and wisdom so they could share the Good News about Jesus with many different people. The Spirit empowered them to spread God's Word, and He still gives us faith and strengthens us to share God's love with others.

Then the day of Trinity arrives. This is usually the day when we recite the Athanasian Creed because it describes so clearly the Three

Persons of the Trinity. Our God is One in Three, in a way we will not fully understand until we are in heaven.

The rest of the year, from early summer to the end of November when Advent begins again, is the season of Pentecost. Throughout Pentecost, God continues to make our faith stronger and make the Church grow. Again, we have the color of green on our altars. We may celebrate special days of saints who have gone before us and have died in the faith.

Hymns for the Church Year

These are hymns for various seasons of the Church Year as found in the hymnal *Lutheran Service Book*.

Advent—Hymns 331–357

Christmas—Hymns 358–393

Epiphany—Hymns 394–412

Lent and **Holy Week**—Hymns 418–456

Easter—Hymns 457–490

Ascension—Hymns 491–495

Pentecost—Hymns 496–503

Trinity—Hymns 504–507

16. What Is the Divine Service?

When Lutherans gather together, we follow an order of worship called the **Divine Service.** The worship service has developed over the centuries. Some parts of it date from the time of the New Testament or even earlier. Each portion of the Divine Service comes from the Bible and is focused on Jesus. Below are the different parts of the Divine Service, what they mean, and where in the Bible they come from.

The Preparation

Invocation

> We call upon God—Father, Son, and Holy Spirit—to bless our worship.
>
> "For through Him we both have access in one Spirit to the Father." (Ephesians 2:18)

Confession and Absolution

> We confess our sins and hear that our sins are forgiven.
>
> "If we confess our sins, He is faithful and just to forgive us our sins and to cleanse us from all unrighteousness." (1 John 1:9)

Service of the Word

Introit (inn-TRO-it) means: "Enter"

> We sing or say verses from the Bible to open the service.
> There are various verses, depending on the day.

Kyrie (KIH-ree-ay) means: "Lord, have mercy"

> We ask the Lord for mercy.
>
> "His mercy is for those who fear Him from generation to generation." (Luke 1:50)

Gloria in Excelsis (GLOW-ree-uh in ex-SHELL-sis) means: "Glory in the highest"

> We sing "Glory to God" with the angels and the whole Church.
>
> "Glory to God in the highest, and on earth peace among those with whom He is pleased!" (Luke 2:14)

Salutation and Collect (KAH-lekt)

The pastor invites us to pray; we pray with him.

"The Lord be with your spirit. Grace be with you." (2 Timothy 4:22)

Old Testament, Epistle, and Holy Gospel Readings

We listen to the Bible readings from the Old and New Testaments.

"Faith comes from hearing, and hearing through the word of Christ." (Romans 10:17)

Creed

We confess our faith in God.

"So everyone who acknowledges Me before men, I also will acknowledge before My Father who is in heaven, but whoever denies Me before men, I also will deny before My Father who is in heaven." (Matthew 10:32–33)

Sermon

We listen to the pastor's message.

"We ask you, brothers, to respect those who labor among you and are over you in the Lord and admonish you." (1 Thessalonians 5:12)

Offering

We give our gifts.

"Each one must give as he has decided in his heart, not reluctantly or under compulsion, for God loves a cheerful giver." (2 Corinthians 9:7)

Prayers

We bring our prayers to God.

"Rejoice always, pray without ceasing, give thanks in all circumstances; for this is the will of God in Christ Jesus for you." (1 Thessalonians 5:16–18)

Offertory

We ask God to keep us from sin and give us joy in Jesus.

"Create in me a clean heart, O God, and renew a right spirit within me. Cast me not away from Your presence, and take not Your Holy Spirit from me. Restore to me the joy of Your salvation, and uphold me with a willing spirit." (Psalm 51:10–12)

Service of the Sacrament

Preface

We begin in the name of the Lord.

"Now may the Lord of peace Himself give you peace at all times in every way. The Lord be with you all." (2 Thessalonians 3:16)

Sanctus (SAHNK-toose) means: "Holy"

We sing or say that God is holy.

"Holy, holy, holy is the LORD of hosts; the whole earth is full of His glory!" (Isaiah 6:3)

Prayer of Thanksgiving and the Lord's Prayer

We thank God for the gifts of God and ask for His blessings.

"Pray then like this: 'Our Father in heaven, hallowed be Your name. Your kingdom come, Your will be done, on earth as it is in heaven. Give us this day our daily bread, and forgive us our debts, as we also have forgiven our debtors. And lead us not into temptation, but deliver us from evil. For if you forgive others their trespasses, your heavenly Father will also forgive you, but if you do not forgive others their trespasses, neither will your Father forgive your trespasses.'" (Matthew 6:9–13)

Words of Institution

The pastor speaks the words of Jesus from the Lord's Supper.

"[Jesus said:] 'This is My body. . . . This is My blood. . . .'" (Matthew 26:26, 28)

Pax Domini means: "Peace be with you"

We share the peace of the Lord.

"Peace be with you." (John 20:19)

Agnus Dei (AHG-noose DAY-ee) means: "Lamb of God"

We sing or say that Jesus is the Lamb of God who takes away our sins.

"The next day he saw Jesus coming toward him, and said, 'Behold, the Lamb of God, who takes away the sin of the world!'" (John 1:29)

Distribution

We receive God's gift of forgiveness in the Lord's Supper.

"[Jesus said:] 'This is My body, which is given for you. Do this in remembrance of Me.'" (Luke 22:19)

Post-Communion Canticle

We thank God for the Lord's Supper and His forgiveness.

"[Simeon said:] 'Lord, now You are letting Your servant depart in peace, according to Your word; for my eyes have seen Your salvation that You have prepared in the presence of all peoples, a light for revelation to the Gentiles, and for glory to Your people Israel.' " (Luke 2:29–32)

Benediction

We receive the blessing of the Lord as we leave the Divine Service.

"The LORD bless you and keep you; the LORD make His face to shine upon you and be gracious to you; the LORD lift up His countenance upon you and give you peace." (Numbers 6:24–26)

Making the Sign of the Cross

In order to help us remember that we were baptized in the name of the Father, Son, and Holy Spirit, we can make the sign of the cross. We "draw" the cross from our forehead to our chest, and then across our shoulders. We can then remember that Jesus died for us on the cross; His love for us was given to us in Baptism. "For Thine is the kingdom and the power and the glory forever and ever. Amen."

What's Next?

Throughout this book, we've discussed the teachings of the Bible and how God loves us in Christ. We've reviewed the Small Catechism, which breaks down the Bible into easy-to-understand sections. We've learned how the hymnal guides us in worship. So what's next? What do we do with all that we now know?

Throughout this book, you've learned about how important it is for you to understand the Bible and to grow in Christ. As God strengthens our faith, we keep learning about Him. And what we have learned and experienced, we share with others.

Pretend that you just found out terrific news, and now you're bubbling with excitement. What do you do with that news? You share it! You tell your friends, your teacher, your coach, even strangers.

This is like the Christian life. When we realize the amazing news about God's love for us in Christ, we can't help but share it. We want to shout it from the mountaintops: "Jesus loves me!" This Good News bubbles up inside us, and we want to tell others. We want to help other people know Jesus. We want to do good things for our parents, brothers and sisters, friends, neighbors, and teachers.

We want people to see this love and faith within us. So we may help our neighbor shovel her sidewalk when it snows. Or we may help Mom with the dishes before she asks. Or we may help a classmate pick up the books that fell out of his locker.

We don't do these things because we're afraid God will be mad at us if we don't. We do them because we are full of the love of God in Christ. A Christian is like an apple tree that can't help but produce apples. The good works we do are like the apples on an apple tree. We can't help but do good things for other people. Think about who you are: a daughter or son, a brother or sister, a neighbor or friend. Do good to those who are closest to you.

And as you keep growing in your faith, "May the God of hope fill you with all joy and peace in believing, so that by the power of the Holy Spirit you may abound in hope" (Romans 15:13).

Glossary

Absolution: The pastor's announcement, with Christ's authority, that you are truly and completely forgiven

actual sin: Things that we think, say, and do that are against God's Law

altar: Piece of furniture in the church, similar to a table, that holds the wine and bread for communion

Baptism: A sacrament, or **Means of Grace**, in which God bestows grace and forgiveness upon the baptized person with water and in the name of the Father, Son, and Holy Spirit

Bible: The holy book that tells about God and what He has done for us; divided into two sections, the Old and New Testaments; also called **God's Word**

canticle: A hymn with words taken directly from the Bible

catechism: A manual used to teach the Christian faith

Church: Community of believers in Christ who come together to receive God's gifts and worship Him

Church Year: The seasons the Church celebrates, based on the life of Christ and the life of the Church

Communion: A sacrament, or Means of Grace, in which God bestows grace and forgiveness upon the communicant through bread and wine and the Words of Institution

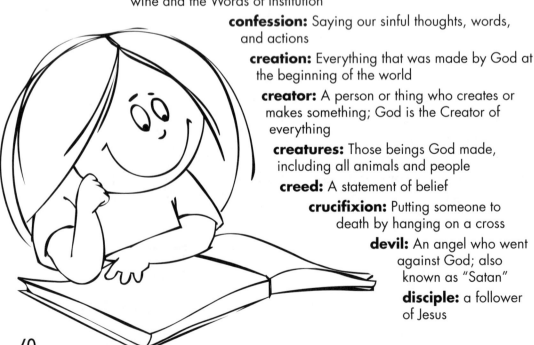

confession: Saying our sinful thoughts, words, and actions

creation: Everything that was made by God at the beginning of the world

creator: A person or thing who creates or makes something; God is the Creator of everything

creatures: Those beings God made, including all animals and people

creed: A statement of belief

crucifixion: Putting someone to death by hanging on a cross

devil: An angel who went against God; also known as "Satan"

disciple: a follower of Jesus

Divine Service: The name for the regular weekly church service that includes the celebration of the **Lord's Supper**

eternal: has always existed; God has no beginning or ending because He has always been and always will be

faith: Belief in God, given and strengthened by the **Holy Spirit**

Father: First Person of the **Trinity**, who made us

font: The container to hold the water for **Baptism**

forgiveness: Not holding someone's wrong against them

God's Word: Holy book that tells about God and what He has done for us; divided into two sections, the Old and New Testaments; also called the **Bible**

Good Friday: The day when we commemorate Jesus' crucifixion

heaven: Life with God forever

hell: Separation from God forever

holy: Set apart for God's special purpose

Holy Spirit: Third Person of the Trinity, who gives us faith

Holy Thursday: The day that Jesus instituted the Lord's Supper; also called Maundy Thursday

Holy Trinity: Word that refers to God as Father, Son, and Holy Spirit

Holy Week: The last week of Lent, during which we commemorate Christ's suffering and death

hymn: A song of praise to God

hymnal: A collection of hymns

inspiration: God's work of leading the people to know which words to use when writing the Bible

Lent: a season of the Church Year when we are sorrowful over our sin

liturgy: The order of the hymns, prayers, and other parts of the **Divine Service**

Lord's Supper: See "Communion"

Luther, Martin: A pastor who lived in the 1500s and helped to make changes in the Church to focus attention on Jesus and His saving work for us

Lutheran: A believer in Christ who follows the teachings of the Bible and the Lutheran Confessions

Means of Grace: the ways by which God creates faith, forgives sin, and provides salvation; Baptism, the Lord's Supper, the Gospel of Jesus Christ

miracle: An action that only God has the power to do, like turning water into wine

New Testament: The second part of the Bible, which tells about Jesus, His work, and the Early Church

Old Testament: The first part of the Bible, which gives the history of God's people from **creation** through the time of the Prophets

omnipotent: A term which describes God as being all powerful, able to do anything

omnipresent: A term which describes God as being always present, or present everywhere at all times

original sin: Our state of being sinful

pastor: Christ's messenger who prays, shares God's Word, and gives us God's gifts

prayer: talking to God

pulpit: podium in a church where a pastor preaches the sermon

repent: acknowledging our sin, feeling sorry for it and wanting forgiveness, and stopping the sinful behavior

Resurrection: The rising of Jesus Christ from the dead

Sacrament: A sacred act that was instituted by God, has a visible element, and offers the forgiveness of sins earned by Christ

saint: A believer in Jesus Christ, baptized and filled with His Spirit, who lives by His teaching

salvation: saved from sin and death through Jesus

Savior: A name for Jesus, who saves us from our sins

sermon: A talk a **pastor** gives, based on a passage from the Bible

sin: A thought, word, or action against God

Son: Second Person of the Trinity, Jesus Christ, who died for us, rose again, and saves us from sin

temptation: Anything that makes us want to sin

Ten Commandments: Laws or rules from God; things that we should do or should not do

Bibliography

Vamosh, Miriam Feinberg, *Daily Life at the Time of Jesus*. Herzlia, Israel: Palphot, Ltd., 2004.

Lutheran Service Book. St. Louis: Concordia Publishing House, 2006.

Luther's Small Catechism with Explanation. St. Louis: Concordia Publishing House, 1986, 1991.

The Lutheran Study Bible. St. Louis: Concordia Publishing House, 2009.

Topical Index

Scripture Index